THE BOTTLENOSE DOLPHIN

BY
**WILLIAM R. SANFORD
CARL R. GREEN**

EDITED BY
DR. HOWARD SCHROEDER, Ph.D.
Professor in Reading and Language Arts
Dept. of Curriculum and Instruction
Mankato State University

CRESTWOOD HOUSE
Mankato, Minnesota

J 599.5
S

LIBRARY OF CONGRESS CATALOGING IN PUBLICATION DATA

Sanford, William R. (William Reynolds).
   The bottlenose dolphin.

   (Wildlife, habits & habitat)
   Includes index.
   SUMMARY: Describes the physical characteristics, habitat, life cycle, and behavior of the best-known kind of dolphin, one frequently seen in marine shows.
   1. Bottlenose dolphin--Juvenile literature. (1. Bottlenose dolphins. 2. Dolphins.) I. Green, Carl R. II. Schroeder, Howard. III. Title. IV. Series.
   QL737.C432S36   1987   599.5'3--dc19   87-19420
   ISBN 0-89686-329-8

International Standard Book Number:	Library of Congress Catalog Card Number:
Library Binding 0-89686-329-8	87-19420

CREDITS

Illustrations:
Cover Photo: Stephen J. Krasemann/DRK Photo
Stephen J. Krasemann/DRK Photo: 5, 6, 8, 14, 16, 24-25
Ed Robinson/Tom Stack & Associates: 10, 29, 44
Brian Parker/Tom Stack & Associates: 13, 26, 30, 34, 41
Kevin Schafer/Tom Stack & Associates: 22
M. Timothy O'Keefe/Tom Stack & Associates: 19
Gary Milburn/Tom Stack & Associates: 33, 37, 38
Andy Schlabach: 45
Graphic Design & Production:
Baker Street Productions, Ltd.

Copyright© 1987 by Crestwood House, Inc. All rights reserved. No part of this book may be reproduced in any form without written permission from the publisher, except for brief passages included in a review. Printed in the United States of America.

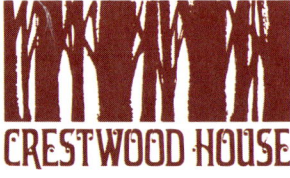

CRESTWOOD HOUSE
Hwy. 66 South, Box 3427
Mankato, MN 56002-3427

TABLE OF CONTENTS

Introduction 4
   Feeding a bottlenose dolphin
Chapter One: The bottlenose dolphin in close-up 9
   A large and lively family
   Dolphins vary in size and color
   A body designed for the ocean
   Coming up for air
   A big brain and keen senses
Chapter Two: The bottlenose dolphin
and its ocean habitat 17
   A wide-ranging habitat
   Fast — but not the fastest
   A diet of fish
   Dolphins like each other
   Dolphins don't fear many predators
   The bottlenose keeps its secrets
Chapter Three: A bottlenose dolphin grows up 27
   A calf is born
   Calves have a lot to learn
   Taking a place in the herd
   Contact with humans
   Cola grows up
Chapter Four: People see
dolphins in many ways 34
   The dolphin in history
   Modern writers also love the dolphin
   Porpoise oil and angry fishermen
   The dolphins put on a show
Chapter Five: What are those dolphins saying? ... 40
   Changing ideas about the dolphin's sounds
   Decoding the dolphin's sounds
   A look into the future
Map: 45
Index/Glossary: 46-47

INTRODUCTION:

"Dad! Guess what!" William burst into the room like a tornado.

Dr. Reynolds looked up from his computer. "Slow down, William," he said. "I know you went to the marineland show today. Was Tom eaten by a shark?"

Tom pushed past his younger brother. "William's excited because the clown let him feed one of the dolphins," he explained.

"Let me tell!" William shouted. "First, the dolphins played basketball and jumped through flaming hoops. Then the clown said a dolphin named Duffy was going to show how high he could jump."

William stopped to catch his breath and Tom took over. "The clown asked for a volunteer," he said. "Then for some reason, he picked William. The two of them climbed up to a little platform twenty feet (6.1 m) above the water. Then the clown gave William a fish and told him to hold it where Duffy could see it."

"I bet William was scared," Dr. Reynolds said.

"No, I wasn't!" William said quickly. "The clown told me that dolphins don't hurt people. I looked down, and I could see Duffy picking up speed. Then he jumped straight up and took the fish right out of my hand. He was looking at me, and he was smiling!

This dolphin puts on a good show at the Miami Seaquarium.

5

The dolphin is a mammal — and a very special one, at that!

He didn't look like a fish at all."

"Of course he didn't look like a fish," Tom said. "The bottlenose dolphins we saw today are mammals that live in the sea. They're related to whales and porpoises."

William looked puzzled. "Dad, that doesn't make sense," he said. "My teacher said that mammals developed on land during the age of dinosaurs. How could a mammal live in the water?"

"You're both right," Dr. Reynolds said. "The first mammals did live on land. But a few mammals went back into the ocean to live. That was thousands of years ago. Scientists call them cetaceans. Their bodies are as well adapted to a life in the water as a lion's is to the land."

"Why would a dolphin go back to the sea?" William asked.

"It wasn't the dolphin that went back," Tom said. "I know, because we studied this in science. An animal called the creodont was the dolphin's great-great grandfather. Creodonts were meat-eaters, but they couldn't compete for prey with the bigger land animals. So they lived mostly on fish that they caught in the water."

"But mammals have four legs, or two legs and two arms," William pointed out. "A dolphin has two flippers and a tail."

"Creodonts developed streamlined bodies that moved easily through the water," Tom said. "Their front legs became flippers and their back legs disappeared. At the same time, their noses moved to the top of their heads to make breathing easier. The dolphin is the result of all those changes."

William looked at his dad. "Are any of today's mammals changing into sea creatures like the dolphin?" he asked.

Dolphins can be found in all of the world's oceans, and even in some rivers.

"Some experts think the sea otter already looks and acts a lot like a seal," Dr. Reynolds said. He stood up and walked to a bookshelf. "Why don't you take a look at this book on cetaceans, William? A boy who feeds dolphins should know more about them."

CHAPTER ONE:

Thousands of years ago, the ancestors of today's whales, dolphins, and porpoises returned to the sea. Naturalists put these modern animals into an order of sea-living mammals known as the *Cetacea*. All are warm-blooded and give birth to live young. Even though they live in the water, the cetaceans must return to the surface to breathe.

The cetaceans are divided into two major groups. One suborder is called the *Mysticeti*. These are the baleen whales, such as the humpback and the blue whale. Instead of teeth, the baleen whales have plates in their mouth like giant combs. The second suborder is known as the *Odontoceti*. These cetaceans have kept their teeth. Typical odontocets are the sperm whales, narwhals, porpoises, and dolphins.

A large and lively family

Dolphins belong to a family called the *Delphinidae*. This large and varied family can be found in all of the world's oceans and in some of its rivers. The *Delphinidae* include killer whales, pilot whales, and about thirty types of dolphins. Although people sometimes mix up their names, dolphins are not porpoises. The true porpoise belongs to a family known as the *Phocoenidae.* It is generally smaller and has a thicker body than a dolphin.

Of all the dolphins, the bottlenose dolphin *(Tursiops truncatus)* is the best known. The dolphins used in marineland shows are often bottlenoses. Many people also remember Flipper, a bottlenose who starred on a popular television show. Naturalists divide the bottlenose into two varieties. One type lives in coastal waters close to the continents. The second prefers an offshore habitat that includes the waters around oceanic islands.

Being a dolphin is a lot of fun!

Dolphins vary in size and color

Bottlenose dolphins vary greatly in size. Adult males (called bulls) range from six to twelve feet (1.8-3.7 m) in length. They weigh between three hundred and five hundred pounds (136-227 kg). One giant bottlenose was measured at almost thirteen feet (4 m) and weighed more than six hundred pounds (272 kg). Females (known as cows) are smaller than bulls. Newborn calves average three and a half feet (1.1 m) in length.

Most bottlenose dolphins are black, slate blue, or grey on the upper half of their bodies. Their dorsal fin, flippers, and tail flukes are the same dark color. The color fades to a lighter shade on the dolphin's sides, and becomes a light grey or pinkish white on the belly. People also report bottlenose dolphins that are all black, all white, or cinnamon-colored.

Experts use several keys to identify the bottlenose. First, they look for the short, stubby beak, which is about three inches (7.6 cm) long. The beak is really the dolphin's mouth. Along with the heavy bones of the skull, it can be used as a ram for driving off predators. Both the upper and lower jaws hold twenty to twenty-six pairs of small, sharp teeth. The mouth curves up in what many people take to be a friendly smile. Another key to spotting a bottlenose is that the chunky front half of the body narrows rapidly behind the dorsal fin.

A body designed for the ocean

The bottlenose dolphin's dorsal fin and tail flukes are vital to its life in the water. The triangular dorsal fin is located at the midpoint of the dolphin's back. Twelve to twenty inches (30 to 51 cm) tall, it acts like a keel to keep the dolphin stable when it's swimming. The two curving tail flukes are set in a horizontal plane. Each fluke is about two feet (61 cm) long. The up-and-down motion of the tail flukes makes it easy for the dolphin to dive and surface. The tail is attached to the dolphin's body by muscles and tissue, not by bone.

The dolphin's bones have adapted, too. An X-ray inspection of the flippers shows the modified arms and fingers of a land animal. In use, the flippers help guide and balance the dolphin. The vertebrae of the neck aren't fused as they are in most dolphins. The bottlenose can turn its head at right angles to its body. Finally, the dolphin's backbone is flexible enough to allow it to bend into an S-shape.

Engineers have studied the bottlenose dolphin's skin in order to design better submarines. They learned that the thin outer skin absorbs water. This, plus the dolphin's smooth shape, helps increase its speed. The dolphin wears a half-inch layer (1.3 cm) of fat (called blubber) beneath the outer skin. Blubber protects the warm-blooded mammal from the ocean cold.

Coming up for air

The bottlenose dolphin breathes through a blowhole located on the top of its head. That location allows the dolphin to breathe without lifting its head out of the water. The name also makes sense, because the dolphin "blows" air and water through the blowhole with great force. The noise can sound like a firecracker exploding. Strong "lips" hold the blowhole tightly shut unless the dolphin is breathing in or blowing out.

When a bottlenose dolphin dives, its body adjusts to a new set of demands. Water pressure drives the air from the lungs into the bronchial tubes. Valves in the bronchial tubes feed oxygen back into the lungs

A bottlenose dolphin breathes through a blowhole on the top of its head.

13

when it's needed. The valves also regulate pressure and trap nitrogen, allowing the dolphin to dive deeply and surface quickly. If the nitrogen was free to form bubbles in the bloodstream, it could kill the dolphin.

The dolphin's blood carries more oxygen than does the blood of land animals. During a dive, most of this oxygen is sent to the brain and heart. At the same time, the dolphin's heart rate slows from one hundred to fifty beats per minute. In a deep dive, a dolphin can stay underwater for five to seven minutes.

A big brain and keen senses

Some naturalists think the bottlenose dolphin's large brain gives it a high level of intelligence. One

The dolphin's brain is highly developed.

reason is that the dolphin's brain is highly developed in the area related to hearing. This may seem strange at first, because the dolphin doesn't have ears on the outside of its body. A pinhole-size external opening leads to a highly developed inner ear.

The inner ear plays a key role in a process called echolocation. The dolphin emits sound waves that are focused by a lens-shaped organ (the melon) in the dolphin's forehead. The waves bounce back from objects in and out of the water. As it listens for these echoes, the dolphin waggles its head from side to side. This gives each ear a "fix" on the object. The echoes reach the inner ear through oil-filled sinus cavities in the lower jaw. From the inner ear, the message goes to the brain to be "decoded." Naturalists have tested echolocation by putting rubber cups over a dolphin's eyes. The "blindfolded" dolphin easily finds food and swims through an underwater maze.

The bottlenose dolphin's eyes work well in and out of water. It can spot a flying fish from beneath the water and leap to catch its prey in the open air. The dolphin's fields of vision overlap, which lets it see in three dimensions. People often notice the dolphin's eyelids. At times it appears as though the animal is winking at its audience! Dolphins may have a sense of smell, but no evidence has been found that it exists.

Because it lacks vocal chords, the dolphin uses its

windpipe and blowhole to make noises. The sounds range from rapid clicks and whistles to snorts, barks, yelps, and grunts. Wherever dolphins swim, they fill their underwater habitat with noisy chatter.

Dolphins can be a very talkative bunch.

CHAPTER TWO:

Most cetaceans ignore our clumsy attempts to share their ocean habitat. That's not true of the bottlenose dolphin. A twelve-year-old New Zealand girl proved that back in 1955. Jill Baker was swimming at Opononi Beach when a young bottlenose surfaced next to her. The dolphin clearly wanted to play. Jill swam with the bottlenose and took a short ride on its back. For the rest of that summer, the animal visited the harbor every day.

The town fell in love with Opo, as the dolphin was called. People came to see her from all over New Zealand. The love affair ended when Opo was killed by some teenagers who were "fishing" with dynamite. That friendship ended in tragedy. But dolphins keep coming back to visit sailors, swimmers, and divers.

A wide-ranging habitat

Bottlenose dolphins live in all but the coldest waters. In the Pacific, they range from Japan and Australia to Southern California and Chile. In the Atlantic, the species is found from Canada to

Argentina and from Norway to South Africa. Bottlenose dolphins also live in the Mediterranean Sea and in the Indian Ocean.

The coastal variety prefers shallow waters of sixty feet (18.3 m) and less. These inshore dolphins often enter harbors, bays, and the mouths of rivers. The warm-water herds generally stay within a limited home territory. The offshore variety roams further and is more widely scattered. These deep-water bottlenose dolphins can often be found in tropical waters.

Fast — but not the fastest

The ancient Greeks believed that the dolphin was the fastest animal of all. That just isn't so. The cheetah has been clocked at seventy miles (113 km) per hour, and a lion can hit fifty miles (80 km) per hour. A dolphin swims fast, but reports of speeds of thirty or forty miles (48-64 km) per hour seem much too high. The U.S. Navy once measured the dolphin's top speed at sixteen miles (26 km) per hour. At that speed, a swimming dolphin develops as much as eight horsepower.

The bottlenose may not be an Olympic sprinter, but it can swim and dive with the best. Each powerful up-and-down stroke of its tail sends it gliding smoothly through the water. In water shows, trained dolphins easily jump twenty feet (6.1 m) or more out of the water. Dolphins also enjoy hitching a ride on the bow wave thrown up by a fast ship.

Dolphins feed mostly near the surface, but they can dive if the fish go deeper. A bottlenose named Tuffy dived to a depth of 984 feet (300 m) in 1966. Tuffy stayed down for seven minutes, but the dolphin likely can extend that time. To supply oxygen to its body, a dolphin exchanges ninety percent of the air in its lungs when it blows. Thus, its bloodstream is fully supplied with fresh oxygen when it dives. By contrast, people exchange only fifteen percent of the air in their lungs when they breathe.

Because the dolphin's bloodstream carries a lot of oxygen, it can stay underwater for long periods of time.

A diet of fish

The bottlenose dolphin catches a variety of fish, squid, and shellfish. Some favorites are mullet, shad, eel, and shrimp. A full-grown dolphin eats about twenty-two pounds (10 kg) of food a day. By human standards, the bottlenose has poor table manners. It swallows small fish whole and bites larger ones in half.

At times, dolphins work together to catch their dinner. The hunt begins with scouts swimming out to find a school of fish. Next, the dolphins line up and swim toward the school. Some leap and splash to scare their prey. When they've rounded up enough fish, the dolphins at the end of the line circle around to close the trap. At that point, discipline breaks down. Each dolphin snaps up as many fish as it can catch.

Bottlenose dolphins tend to go where the fishing is good. Some Atlantic-coast dolphins follow the Gulf Stream north in the spring. They stay close to shore, where the shallow waters are filled with fish. By summer, they've reached the Gulf of Maine or the Grand Banks off Nova Scotia. When fall brings colder weather, the herds turn southward to warmer waters. Bottlenose dolphins who live in warm waters may not migrate at all. They stay in a home range as small as ten miles (16 km) in length.

Dolphins like each other

If you spot one bottlenose dolphin, you're likely to see several more. Dolphins live in herds of four to ten animals. These small herds are usually part of a larger herd that can vary from forty to two hundred dolphins. A small herd usually has several cows, their young calves, and a bull. The bull guards the herd, and makes sure the calves obey orders. Each animal has its own place in the herd's pecking order. Generally, larger dolphins dominate smaller ones.

Dolphins are loving and playful. They often rub together, or touch each other with their flippers and beaks. If the spirit moves them, the dolphins leap and turn somersaults. If one dolphin finds a bit of seaweed, it may start a game of keep-away. In coastal areas, surfers are sometimes surprised to see dolphins riding the waves only a few feet away.

Dolphins do most of their feeding during the day. They sleep for several hours each night, and nap for an hour or so after a heavy feeding. The cows sleep with their blowholes just above the surface. Males sleep a foot or so below the surface. They rise to the surface to breathe every few minutes, their tails beating slowly to keep their position. The herd stays close together during sleep periods as protection against attack.

Dolphins don't fear many predators

Bottlenose dolphins have little to fear from the ocean's predators. Only sharks and killer whales are a real danger to the calves. If a shark comes too close to the herd, the bulls charge it at high speed and ram it with their heads and beaks. After several rammings, the shark usually swims off to find easier prey. Even so, more than half of the dolphins checked in one study carried scars from shark bites.

If dolphins aren't careful, they may be bitten by sharks when feeding in the same area.

Most dolphins are bitten when they're competing with sharks for the same fish.

Bottlenose dolphins face a greater danger from what naturalists call "stranding" or "beaching." Some strandings are accidents, as when a dolphin is caught in rocks and left behind by a changing tide. Dried out by the sun, the dolphin goes into shock and dies. At other times, an entire herd may beach itself for no apparent reason. Naturalists blame parasites that damage the dolphin's sensitive inner ear for some of these disasters. Like people, dolphins also suffer from pneumonia, cancer, heart disease, and stomach upsets.

The bottlenose doesn't seem to fear people, and that is the greatest danger of all. Thousands of dolphins drown each year when they get tangled in fishing nets. Others are killed by speeding powerboats. Pollution is a silent killer. Oil spills, pesticide runoff, and sewage often poison the water and the animals that live in it.

The bottlenose keeps its secrets

Naturalists say it's much easier to study land animals than to study the cetaceans. For example, how long does a bottlenose live? The ancient Greeks said they live for thirty years. That study was made

The ancient Greeks believed the dolphin could live for up to thirty years.

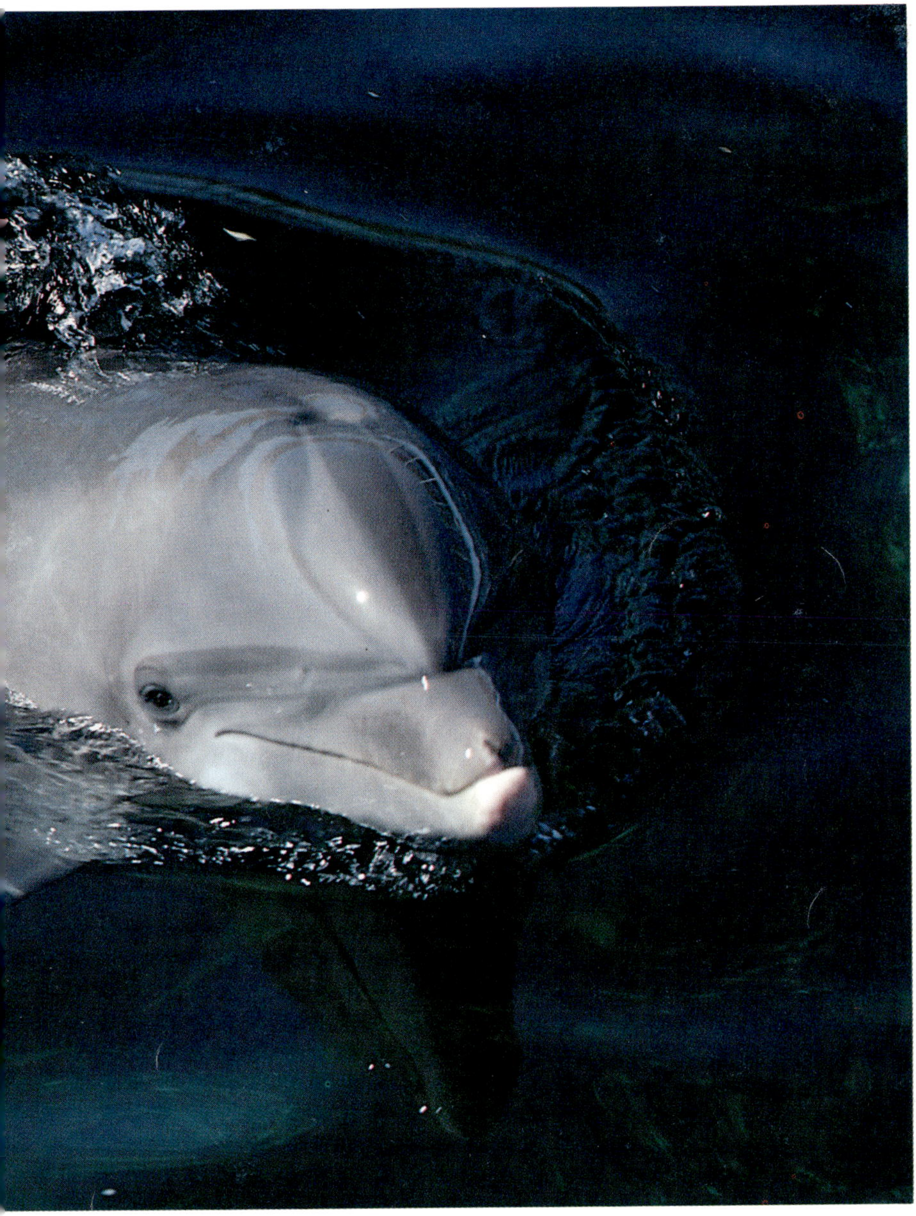

two thousand years ago, but no one has come up with a better estimate. Despite the scientists' handicaps, experts have learned some interesting facts about the life cycle of the dolphin.

The dolphin's way of life has always interested scientists.

CHAPTER THREE:

The water of the tidal lagoon lies still and warm beneath the bright sun of early May. A team of naturalists has been studying the marine life along this remote North Carolina coastline. They aren't expecting the drama that takes place that day.

A bottlenose dolphin cow swims slowly into the lagoon. She has been carrying her calf for a year, and the time of birth is near. A second cow, called an "auntie," follows close behind. Offshore, the rest of the herd circles, watching for sharks and barracuda. The cows see a naturalist in scuba gear, but they don't sense any danger.

A calf is born

The female calf enters her watery world with her tail first. If she emerged headfirst, she might drown before reaching the surface. The newborn dolphin is small for a bottlenose, only three feet (1 m) long and twenty-five pounds (11.3 kg). As soon as the calf is free, she unfolds her tail flukes and swims to the surface. The movement breaks the umbilical cord and allows the calf to take her first breath.

The mother dolphin and the auntie swim close

and support the newborn dolphin. They whistle softly, as if soothing the calf. The calf responds with her own shaky whistling sounds. Then the cow turns on her side so the calf can nurse. Instinct tells the calf what to do. She presses against her mother's belly to find one of her teats. The teats lie hidden in "pockets" to reduce drag when the cow is swimming. The calf forms a tube with her upper jaw and tongue, but she doesn't have to suck. The cow squirts the rich milk into the calf's mouth. She'll nurse every twenty minutes or so for the first few weeks.

The naturalist is filming the birth. Watching the calf nurse, she decides to call her Cola. "Her beak is just the size and shape of a soft-drink bottle," she tells herself.

Calves have a lot to learn

When Cola is swimming strongly, the two cows rejoin the herd. The dominant bull leads them northward. Cola has a lot to learn. Her swimming motion is awkward, like a baby learning to walk. In addition, she hasn't mastered the rhythm of swimming and breathing. Sometimes she sticks her head too far out of the water. At other times, she opens her blowhole too soon and seawater rushes in. Cola chokes and splutters as she tries to clear her windpipe.

A little calf stays close to its mother.

Cola's mother keeps her calf close to her. If Cola strays to chase a mullet, the cow quickly nudges her back. Today, Cola is feeling frisky. She refuses to get back in line. The cow slaps her with a flipper and Cola gets the message. If the mother dolphin goes off to hunt, she leaves Cola with a "babysitter."

When the herd is traveling, Cola sometimes rides her mother's back by holding on to her dorsal fin. Naturalists think this behavior may account for one of the well-known stories about dolphins. Hard facts are few, but the stories all say that dolphins save drowning children by carrying them back to shore.

The dolphins fill the water with their whistles and clicks. As Cola matures, the sounds form pictures inside her head. One set of sounds tells her to beware of a large, striped fish that shadows the herd now and then. The other dolphins know that tiger sharks prey on careless calves.

Taking a place in the herd

At two months, Cola has doubled her birth weight. She will continue to nurse until she's eighteen months old. Her first solid food comes from

After eighteen months, a dolphin calf stops nursing and begins its adult diet, which includes fish, shrimp, and eels.

scraps dropped by the other dolphins. Cola watches the others catch fish before she chases mullet and whitefish for herself. At first, she misses every time. But the sound pictures formed in her head by echolocation get sharper. Finally, she makes her first catch. The small shad tastes great!

The largest bull swims guard around Cola's herd. When he gives the danger signal, the herd closes into a tight circle. The calves and their mothers stay in the center. At other times, the calves play chasing games. They've learned to leap into the air and to fall back with a great splash. The adult dolphins don't mind the fun and games — until Cola scares off a school of fish. For that, the dominant bull gives her a sharp nip.

As the dolphins move northward, they join other dolphin herds. Their peaceful nature shows in their friendly meetings. The females are free to change herds if they wish. The bulls seldom fight, unless they think another bull is cutting into their group of females. Young bulls swim off to form all-male herds.

The dolphins also help each other. Off Rhode Island one day, a young bull is stunned when he's grazed by a speedboat. Quickly, two females swim under and hold him up by the flippers. They support him at the surface until he can swim normally again.

Contact with humans

Cola has learned a new trick. When she finds a school of fish close to shore, she herds them right up to the beach. Then she snaps up the stranded fish and takes the next wave back to deeper water. But she misjudges the tide this time. The waves leave her stranded. She flops and turns, but her body feels terribly heavy without water to support it. Cola's mother hears her distress signals, but there's nothing she can do.

Suddenly, Cola sees strange creatures around her. A party of children have found the stranded dolphin. Two of them splash water on Cola while the others run for help. A lifeguard shows them how to roll her over onto a blanket. Then they work together to drag her back into the water. Thanks to the quick action, Cola hasn't gone into shock. She swims in circles for a moment, and then heads back to the herd. The children cheer her on her way.

Cola grows up

By the time she's five, Cola is a mature bottlenose cow. It's April, and she's ready to mate. A handsome, slate-blue bull swims alongside her. The pair stay close to each other for a week or more. Sometimes they stroke each other with their flippers. At other times, Cola rushes away and leaps out of the water. But she always comes back to the waiting bull.

After the bull mates with Cola, he drifts away. Cola stays close to the other cows. The females who have young calves won't mate this year. Raising a dolphin calf is a full-time task. In the years to come, Cola will raise five healthy calves. She's lucky, for she survived her contact with humans. Dolphins have never learned that humans can be enemies as well as friends.

Not all contact with people is friendly. In a street market in Peru, the dolphin's cousin, the porpoise, is used as food.

CHAPTER FOUR:

Ancient people told many stories of dolphins that saved humans from drowning. In one Greek myth, dolphins saved Icadius, the son of the god Apollo Delphinius. To show his thanks, Icadius built a temple to his father at Delphi. The word "dolphin" comes to us from the name of the god and his city.

Similarly, a Roman myth tells about Neptune, god of the sea. In the story, a dolphin brought the beautiful Amphitrite to Neptune to be his wife. The grateful god honored the dolphin by hanging some new stars in the southern sky — the Dolphin constellation.

If dolphins are treated right, they can become very special and loyal friends.

The dolphin in history

Early history books add more tales about the dolphins. Pliny the Elder wrote of some bottlenoses who herded fish into the nets of village fishermen. The partnership increased the catch for both humans and dolphins. Pliny also reported that a dolphin once lived in a lake near Naples, Italy. The dolphin made friends with a boy who was kind to him. In the story, the dolphin carried the boy to school each day on its back. Pliny wrote that the dolphin died of sorrow after the boy fell ill and died.

Ancient kings and queens decorated their temples and palaces with pictures of dolphins. The dolphins are shown as friendly, playful creatures. Some people thought they were humans who had taken the form of sea creatures. Others saw them as gods who brought good luck to people who were kind to them.

Modern writers also love the dolphin

Modern writers are more likely to marvel at the dolphin's behavior. In *Moby Dick,* Herman Melville called for three cheers for the "lucky" dolphins.

"Their presence is generally hailed with delight by the mariner," he wrote. "Full of fine spirits, they... come from the breezy billows to windward. They are the lads that always live before the wind."

Author Loren Eisley wasn't sure that people are smarter than the dolphin. Humans have hands to go with their brains, he said. As a result, they've just about wrecked our planet. Dolphins have brains, but lack hands. Maybe they are geniuses at doing nothing, Eisley suggested. The dolphin watches and wonders, but lives at peace with its ocean home.

Porpoise oil and angry fishermen

In the 1800's, "porpoise fishing" was almost as common as whaling. Atlantic-coast fishermen killed dolphins and porpoises for the oil in their blubber. In 1884, boats from one factory netted and killed 1,268 bottlenose dolphins. The factory made extra profits from the oil in the dolphin's lower jaw cavities. Watchmakers paid high prices for this "jaw oil."

Most fishing for dolphins stopped when the price of oil fell. In 1972, the federal government passed laws to protect all cetaceans in U.S. waters. Small cetaceans are fair game in other parts of the world,

Although most countries have outlawed the killing of dolphins and porpoises, the practice continues in some areas. Shown above are porpoises in a Peru marketplace.

however. Fishermen still kill dolphins off the coasts of Turkey, India, and South America.

Dolphins often appear where commercial fishing boats are working. Sometimes they get tangled in the nets and drown before they can be released. A bigger problem develops when fishermen accuse dolphins of eating the fish they're trying to catch. In 1978, this argument led to a terrible slaughter. Japanese fishing boats herded a thousand dolphins and false killer whales into a bay at Iki Island. Then the workers killed them all. Despite protests from around the world, another eight hundred were killed in 1980.

Dolphins and porpoises are sometimes killed by fishermen, who accuse them of eating the fish they're trying to catch.

The dolphins put on a show

The killings seem more like murder when you see trained bottlenoses in action. The first Marineland opened on Mantanzas inlet in Florida in 1938. Dolphins were captured and kept for display. As time went by, the dolphins thought up their own tricks. They jumped for food and played catch with shells from the bottom of the tank. When someone gave them an innertube, they used it for a dozen different games.

Trainers began coaching the dolphins. They used bits of fish to reward the behaviors they wanted. The dolphins responded to hand signals, spoken commands, and whistles. Pretty soon they were playing basketball and football. One learned to pull a surfboard and its rider. A chorus line of dolphins even put on a hula dance while standing on their tails!

Tricks are fun to watch, but scientists have other questions to ask. They wonder at the dolphin's social behavior, and at its swimming skills. Most of all, they listen to the sounds the dolphin makes. Are those clicks, whistles, and squeals part of a dolphin language? If so, perhaps we can learn to talk to the bottlenose.

CHAPTER FIVE:

The last few years have seen some amazing experiments with language. Using sign language, scientists have been "talking" to chimpanzees and gorillas. A gorilla named Koko used signs to ask for a kitten to keep as a pet.

In some ways, great apes are very similar to people. It seems natural that they might use language like ours. But what about dolphins? These friendly cetaceans aren't like we are at all. They can't make signs, because they don't have hands. More to the point, they live in a different environment. Even so, some scientists think bottlenose dolphins are highly intelligent. They're working hard to learn the dolphin's language.

Changing ideas about the dolphin's sounds

In ancient times, people thought that animals who lived in the water couldn't make any sounds. That changed when scientists studied the cetaceans more carefully. It became clear that whales and dolphins use a wide variety of sounds for communication and echolocation. Humpback whales sing long, lovely songs. The dolphin's rapid clicks and whistles are as varied as the sounds of any human language.

With that insight, some people went too far. Newspapers printed stories that said dolphins could learn human speech. People imagined that bottlenoses would talk in a high-pitched, Donald Duck voice. These dreams turned out to be science fiction.

Scientists began to listen to the dolphin's natural sounds. Some sounds (the whistles) are clearly meant to carry a message from one dolphin to another. Other sounds (the clicks) are used in echolocation. The bottlenose can detect sounds that range between 150 and 200,000 cps (cycles per second). Your own ears hear sounds between twenty and twenty thousand cps. Thus, we can hear some of the dolphins' sounds — and they can hear almost all of ours.

A dolphin's range of sound is many times greater than that of a human being.

Decoding the dolphin's sounds

Dolphins seem to use their whistles in the same way we use words. Naturalists have taped hours of these "conversations." Taping the whistles is easy. The hard part is decoding them. The experts don't know whether the sounds stand for letters, words, or ideas. One far-out theory suggests that the whistles are the bottlenose version of a television broadcast. After all, we send signals through the air that our television sets turn into pictures. If this theory is correct, electronics experts might one day build a "dolphin television set." The set would turn the whistles into pictures we could see.

Other researchers are trying something different. They are trying to develop a computer-based system that humans and dolphins can use together. This plan starts with the fact that dolphins seem to want to talk to us. They make many of their sounds within the range humans can hear. Similarly, they quickly learn to obey spoken commands from their trainers.

The first step will be to program a computer to translate human speech into sounds that dolphins can hear. Next, the dolphin's "speech" must be translated into language people can understand. A powerful computer will then be programmed to do a high-speed, two-way translation. In a way, it will be like using a computer to translate Spanish into English and back again. The big problem is that no one knows how to speak Dolphin.

A look into the future

In this high-tech age, many things seem possible. Imagine a future chat between a scientist and a dolphin:

"How do you feel about talking to humans?" the scientist asks. He's speaking into a microphone hooked up to a computer. The computer quickly translates the words into dolphin sounds.

An underwater speaker broadcasts a series of whistles and clicks to the dolphin. The dolphin listens and whistles a reply. The computer program "reads" the whistles and translates them.

"It's about time," answers the bottlenose. "Dolphins have been trying to talk to you ever since your ancestors learned how to swim. We've watched you kill our cousins and pollute the water we live in. Why don't you relax and enjoy life like we do?"

Why hasn't someone made a setup like this? For one thing, it will cost millions of dollars. And there's no guarantee that this plan, or any other, will work. But think of the joy we'll feel if we do make a breakthrough!

Maybe — just maybe — you'll be able to read this book to a dolphin some day. Then you can ask, "Did the authors get the facts straight?"

Talking with dolphins is a distant and wonderful dream.

MAP:

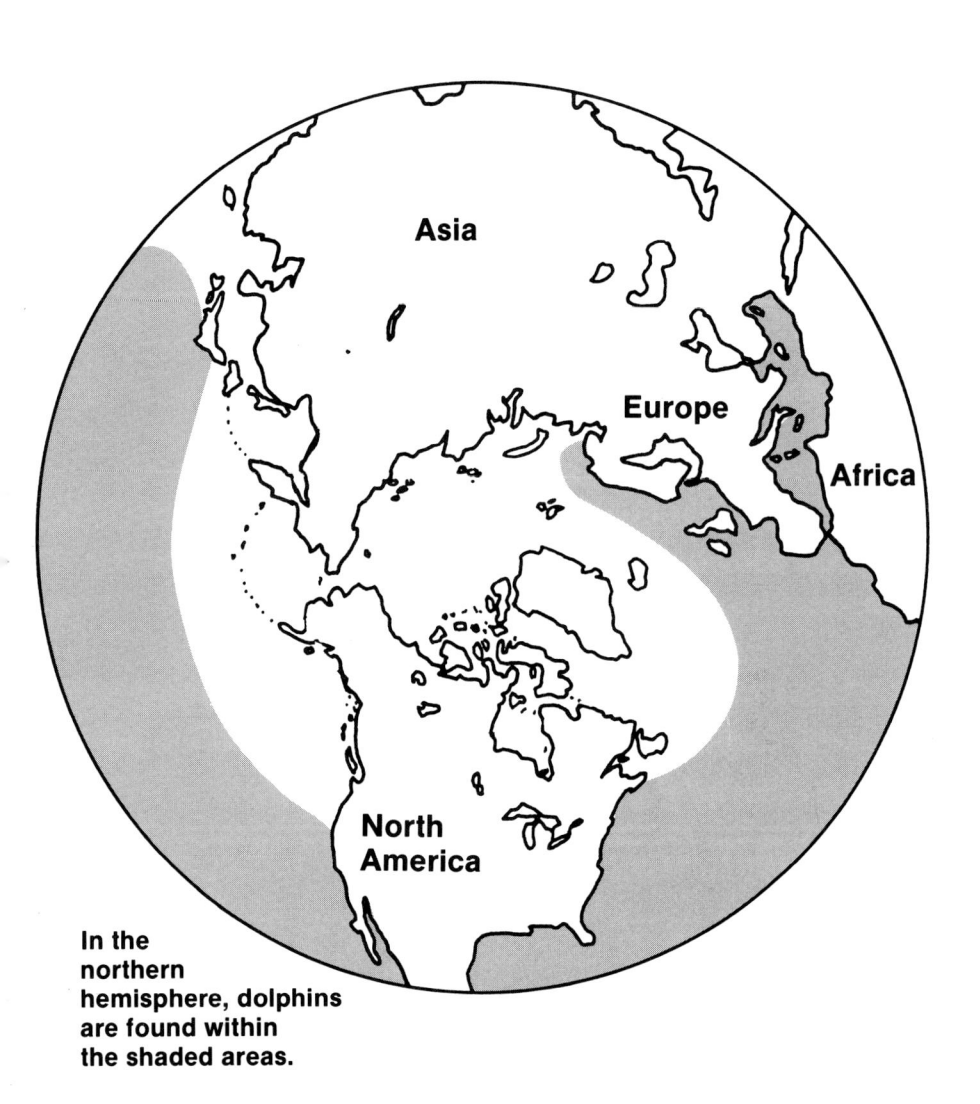

In the northern hemisphere, dolphins are found within the shaded areas.

45

INDEX/GLOSSARY:

AUNTIES 27 — *Bottlenose dolphin cows that help other cows give birth and take care of their calves.*

BEAK 11, 22, 28 — *The dolphin's projecting mouth and jaws, which look a little like a bird's beak.*

BEHAVIOR 19, 21, 28, 29, 39

BLOWHOLE 13, 21, 28 — *A "nose" located on top of the dolphin's head. A dolphin breathes through its blowhole.*

BLUBBER 12, 36 — *The layer of insulating fat that lies just under the outer skin of a dolphin.*

BULL 11, 21, 22, 28, 31, 32, 33 — *An adult male bottlenose dolphin.*

CALF 11, 21, 22, 27, 28, 29, 30, 31, 33 — *A young male or female bottlenose dolphin.*

CETACEANS 6, 7, 9, 17, 23 — *A family of sea-living mammals that includes whales, porpoises, and dolphins.*

COLOR 11

COW 11, 21, 27, 28, 29, 32, 33 — *An adult female bottlenose dolphin.*

CREODONTS 7 — *Ancient mammals that fed on fish.*

DIET 20, 30, 31

DORSAL FIN 11, 12, 29 — *A stabilizing fin that grows at the midpoint of a bottlenose dolphin's back.*

ECHOLOCATION 15 — *When a dolphin finds its food by sending out sounds and "reading" the echo that bounces back.*

ENEMIES 22, 23

ENVIRONMENT 23, 40 — *All of the natural forces and conditions that affect the life of a particular species.*

FLIPPERS 11, 12, 29, 31, 33 — *Flat, paddle-like limbs that the dolphin uses for guidance and balance.*

FLUKES 11, 12, 27 — *The two halves of a dolphin's tail.*

HABITAT 10, 16, 17 — *The place where an animal makes its home.*

MATING 32, 33

MELON 15 — *An organ in the dolphin's forehead that focuses the soundwaves used in echolocation.*

NATURALIST 9, 10, 23, 27, 28, 29, 42 — *A scientist who studies plants and animals.*

PECKING ORDER 21 — *The order of dominance in a herd of bottlenose dolphins.*

INDEX/GLOSSARY:

PHYSICAL CHARACTERISTICS 11, 12, 13, 15
PREDATOR 11, 22 — *An animal that lives by preying on other animals.*
RANGE 17, 18
SENSES 15
SIZE 11, 27
SOUNDS 16, 28, 30, 39, 40, 41, 42, 43
STRANDING 23 — *When a cetacean is trapped on land and can't return to the sea.*
TEATS 28 — *The nipples of a bottlenose dolphin cow. The cow squirts milk from her teats into the mouth of her calf.*
UMBILICAL CORD 27 — *The cord that connects an unborn calf to its mother. The umbilical cord carries food and oxygen to the calf during the months before birth.*
WEIGHT 11, 27, 30

WILDLIFE
HABITS & HABITAT

READ AND ENJOY THE SERIES:

If you would like to know more about all kinds of wildlife, you should take a look at the other books in this series.

You'll find books on bald eagles and other birds. Books on alligators and other reptiles. There are books about deer and other big-game animals. And there are books about sharks and other creatures that live in the ocean.

In all of the books you will learn that life in the wild is not easy. But you will also learn what people can do to help wildlife survive. So read on!